T0148758

Everything You Need To Know

THE MIND

Everything You Need To Know
The Mind

ASPEN
BOOKS

© Aspen Books, 2018

First published in 2018.

A catalogue record for this book is available from the British Library.

ISBN: 978-1-912456-05-5

Published by Aspen Books, an imprint of
Pillar Box Red Publishing Ltd.

Everything You Need To Know

THE MIND

ASPEN
BOOKS

Niki Smith

Contents

INTRO

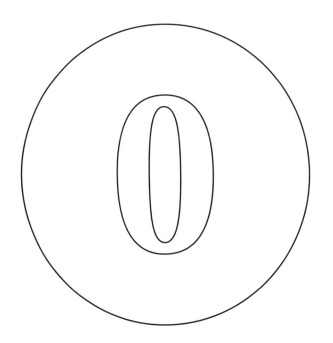

Have you ever wondered about wondering? Thought about thinking? Or even considered your consciousness? How exactly does that lump of grey and white matter sitting inside the skull help us to make sense of the world and our place within it?

The mind is often described as the centre of what it is to be a human, the bit of us that does our thinking and that most of us would describe as 'me'.

But what is that thing we cannot see but controls our faculties helping us to reason, think, judge, speak, and retain information that we can call on when we need it and sometimes even when we don't?

The mind tells us who we are, and who we think we are. It is the 'us' that engages with the world, allows us to reach out to our environment and the people around us, and lets us know what we think about everything we encounter both consciously and subconsciously.

How do we decide if we are a cat person, a dog person, or someone who prefers stick insects? What are we doing when we 'prefer' anyway? How do we know we like modern art or classical music? How do we know when we love someone enough to settle down with them forever more? Or even, how do we know when we want to run screaming in the opposite direction?

Our mind is the thing that lets us do all the wonderful things that we have decided make us Human Beings, it lets us make both good and bad choices and functions like a tiny Jiminy Cricket on our shoulders helping us to get on with the world and everyone in it.

The mind is also probably the number one bit of us that we most fear going wrong. Throughout time, the idea of losing our minds has struck fear into the very core of our being. Somehow losing what makes us quintessentially 'us' is scarier than the worst physical illness.

And what about our pets? The animals around us? Do they have the same thought processes as their human companions on the planet? Do dogs dream? Do Giraffes? Do animals understand the world just as we do, or in some other way we haven't even thought of?

And with the equally compelling and repelling rise of Artificial Intelligence, is it really possible to teach machines how to think? In a hundred years from now, will your computer know what you need before you've even thought about it?

The mind is a fascinating place to be, where we dream our wildest dreams, forge ambition, and appreciate the beauty of the world we live in. Join us as we explore everything you need to know about the mind.

OVERVIEW OF THE BRAIN

Our brains are truly magical things. What is essentially a three pound lump of matter made up of billions of neurons and nerve fibres – which form our grey and white matter respectively – is responsible for many aspects of the body's automatic functions. When it comes to motor control, sensory processing, the regulation of our heartbeat, breathing, hormone production, temperature and sleep, language, emotion, and cognition, the brain is where it's all at.

The brain, after all, is what makes you capable of reading this book.

As the control centre of the nervous system, the brain governs most of the body's activities and responds, processes, and integrates all the data it receives from the world around it through our senses.

At around 2% of an adult's total body weight, the human brain is the largest of all the vertebrates relative to size. Of course, the size of the human brain in comparison to other animals is what makes us capable of speech, planning, logic, and abstract thought – the very things that separate us from our animal brethren.

A little anatomy

The brain is made up of three main sections, the cerebrum, the brainstem, and the cerebellum. The cerebrum is the biggest of the three sections and is divided into two halves called cerebral hemispheres. Each hemisphere is then subdivided into four lobes: the frontal, temporal, parietal, and occipital lobes.

The frontal lobe gives us self-control, planning, reasoning and abstract thought. The temporal lobe processes sensory input and gives us language, communication, and visual memory. The parietal lobe helps us to navigate and gives us spatial awareness, and touch. And the fourth lobe, the occipital lobe, gives us vision. It is the cerebrum and its lobes that are in charge of everything our bodies are thinking and feeling.

The cerebellum, on the other hand, works to regulate movement and gives us posture, balance, coordination and speech helping us to control our muscles in a smooth and measured way – at least, most of the time.

Finally, the brainstem allows the brain to communicate with the rest of the body and controls essential automatic functions like breathing, swallowing, heart rate, blood pressure, consciousness, and sleep. Another way is to think of the brain stem as a motorway that connects the city (the brain), and the suburbs (the rest of the body).

But just how does all this information transferring happen? How does the brain tell all the separate bits of our bodies what to do and when to do it?

The most important foundations of the human nervous system are the neurons. These are cells that communicate information from the brain to the body and can be specialised according to the job they do. Sensory neurons carry information from the sensory receptor cells for example, whereas motor neurons tell the muscles what the brain wants them to do.

The 86 billion neurons working away to make you who you are, are connected by trillions of synapses. These connections squirrel away tirelessly to transport the information contained by neurons to other neurons via neurotransmitters – and this continues while you think you are at rest. Even as you are reading this sentence, your synapses are busy transporting the new information you are acquiring. In other words, as Joseph LeDoux would say: "You are your synapses. They are who you are".[1]

So now that we understand a little bit about the brain and its anatomy, how do we work out where the *mind* is located?

Where is the mind?

The simple answer is, there really isn't a simple answer. While we can all roughly agree that the mind is certainly *in* the brain, its exact location remains a mystery. In study after study utilising brain imaging technology, scientists have seen the brain at work as it functions. The futuristic-sounding fMRI works by charting increased blood flow across the brain essentially lighting up certain areas because: "active neurons consume oxygen, the brain compensates by sending oxygen-rich blood their way; fMRI can map areas of neuronal function by tracking the flow of oxygenated haemoglobin."[2] Perhaps the most well known brain imaging study is Enigma, the world's largest on-going brain mapping project, carried out by almost 900 researchers across 39 countries with 30,000 subjects. Enigma has produced valuable data and images and continuously works to bring together scientists interested in brain structure, function, and disease.[3]

While cognitive neuroscientists have come to the understanding that the mind functions like a network across many parts of the brain, this area of science is still relatively new and constantly developing.

And where does all this incredible data and imaging lead us? Well,

1. https://faculty.washington.edu/chudler/synapse.html

2. http://kavli.yale.edu/news/article.aspx?id=6982

3. http://enigma.ini.usc.edu

according to one scientist, David Rudrauf at the University of Iowa, rather than trying to locate a specific area responsible, it might be better to think of the mind: "like a virtual machine running on distributed computers, with brain resources allocated in a flexible manner"[4]. In other words, our minds are made up of a set of characteristics that can be found in lots of different areas of the brain that work together to produce what we think of specifically as 'the mind'.

So in conclusion, what we can say at this point is that the mind is the whole of the brain at work – controlling our bodily functions, responding to the world around us, interacting with other people, making judgements, dreaming, and making each of us self-aware. The mind is who we think we are, what makes us unique, and what makes us capable of so many wonderful, and amazing things.

IMPORTANT BITS OF THE BRAIN

Left hemisphere

The left hemisphere of your brain controls the right side of your body and is a very logical being. It is responsible for everything related to the rational and logical such as speech, reasoning, language, writing and number skills.

Right hemisphere

The right hemisphere controls the left-hand side of your body and gives your creativity. Imagination, intuitivity, music and 3D shape awareness all come from your right brain.

---

4. https://www.newscientist.com/article/dn22205-location-of-the-mind-remains-a-mystery/

Frontal lobe

This is the most evolved bit of the human brain and is responsible for reasoning, emotions, self-consciousness and planning.

Parietal lobe

This part of the brain helps you to exist in time and space as well as processing environmental and sensory information.

Thalamus

This little nugget sorts out your sensory inputs so that some of it can be ignored and some of it can reach the deeper parts of your brain.

Hypothalamus

The hypothalamus makes sure your brain and your hormones all get on with each other nicely. It is responsible for all sorts of body functions like body temperature and also controls your body weight and your appetite.

Reticular formation

This is a network of nerve pathways in the brainstem that connects the spinal cord, the cerebrum and the cerebellum. Most important-ly, this doodad keeps you at one with gravity which is very useful indeed.

Amygdala

The amygdala might only be the size and shape of an almond, but this little nubbin packs a serious punch – literally. The amygdala is responsible for how we respond to things we are scared of and gives us not only a sense of fear but also a memory of fear as well.

Hippocampus

The horse-shoe shaped hippocampus lets us store long-term memories and helps us to remember people and where we have put our stuff. Without one, we wouldn't know who our friends are or where we live.

A BRIEF
HISTORY OF
THE MIND

But first, a brief note on evolution. Billions of years ago, Earth was populated with primitive organisms. These organisms existed on a causation basis and as such, there was no 'mind' in existence, our forebears simply reacted as and when according to whatever else they came into contact with. Fast forward billions of years, and thanks to the amazing powers of evolution, some organisms developed more sophisticated reactions to their environments, as yet more time passed (and we're talking billions of years again), these processes became more and more refined until we ended up as the thinking, walking, good-looking creatures that we are today.

Homo Sapiens

Homo Sapiens, or the modern Human Beings we know and love, as distinct from their primate forbears, first arrived on the scene in Africa some 130,000 years ago which means we've been here for a piffling amount of time when you think about it.

Prior to this, around 5-7 million years ago, there were other species of hominids: Australopithecus afarensis, Homo habilis, Homo erectus, Homo neanderthalensis. But it turns out that these guys just didn't have any sticking power.

The traits of human intelligence such as: empathy, theory of mind, mourning, ritual, the use of symbols and tools are exhibited by the great apes. Similarly, the Neanderthals were the first species of hominids to wear clothes, homo erectus conquered fire, and the first human-like apes, Homo habilis, were the earliest users of stone tools.

So what makes us different?

What separates Homo sapiens from our hominid cousins is the size of our brains, skull shape and behaviour. Some people might argue we are different because of the relative lack of hair covering our bodies but then again, some people might just think otherwise.

The biggest aspect of our behaviour and development that marks the distinction between us and everyone who came before us, is our use of language. Language is intimately connected to the mind as it is the way in which we can communicate our ability to think, dream, plan and connect.

In relation to this, symbolic behaviour such as cave art, tools, statues and rudimentary jewellery is thought to reveal our early capacity for abstract and symbolic thinking. In other words, around 30,000 years ago, the first signs of what we understand as modern human behaviours became apparent.

Social brains

There are a number of theories as to why humans developed what we understand as intelligence. One such theory, the Social Brain, says that human intelligence came about as a means of surviving in large social groups. In other words, our intelligence evolved as a result of living in complex communities, rather than as a reaction to the environment, and the necessity of being able to understand other peoples' thoughts and emotions. Incidentally, this theory, first put forward by anthropologist Robin Dunbar, is also the reason why you probably have around 150 people (Dunbar's Number) that you would call a friend – go on, check your social network, you know you want to.

Other theories such as Social Exchange Theory, sexual selection, and group selection are all grounded in the idea that we need to get on with those around us in order to achieve the best outcome: survival of the human race. Essentially, a rather nice way to say we are intelligent because we need to get on with our friends and to do so means we need to understand their thoughts and feelings. In other, 'other' words, our minds are inextricably linked to our very survival.

Now that we've established a little bit of evolutionary foundation, how did our ancestors think about the mind? Did our Stone Age brethren have the same social anxieties as we do? Did the Egyptians feel the need for closure after a long relationship? And did the Romans need to chill out with a nice glass of wine after a hard day at work?

What history tells us about the mind

Ancient history (60,000 bc – 650 ad)

Ancient History includes the Stone age and the Shang Dynasty, but we're going to explore what the Egyptians did for us.

The Egyptians

We have an awful lot to thank the Ancient Egyptians for. Ramps, levers, paper, toothpaste, calendars, breath mints, Maths, and of course, awesome eyeliner, all originated in Ancient Egypt. So it stands to reason that our very advanced Egyptian friends would have something to say about the mind, and so they did.

Ancient Egyptians believed in a strong connection between thoughts and feelings and believed that both originated in the heart. For this reason, symptoms of depression were described as *fever in the heart*, or *debility of the heart*.

The Ancient Greeks

Hah, what didn't they give us? Democracy, art, the Olympics, medicine, law, science, philosophy, alarm clocks, maps, and of course, the umbrella.

The Ancient Greeks were the first civilization to realise that the brain understands sensory information and was responsible for thought and memory. The Greeks again understood illness to be a combination of psychic and physical pain. They were also the first to really get into the mind and all its facets. The first people to think about thinking how and why we think, to understand knowledge, reality, and existence can be found here. Thales, Pythagoras, Socrates, Plato and Aristotle are all considered to be the founding fathers of this academic field of study we know and love today.

The Romans

The Romans gave us fast food, advertising, plumbing and sanitation, the Julian calendar, Latin, bureaucracy, and extremely straight roads.

The Romans also gave us the very first experimental physiologist, Galen, who believed that the frontal lobes of the brain were the "seat of the soul".[5] It is at this point in history that we first realise that the brain deals with sensory input and controls our motor functions.

---

5. https://plato.stanford.edu/entries/galen/

The Middle Ages (500 – 1500)

Whilst the Greeks, Romans and everyone else had been busy revolutionising the modern world and doing a serious amount of investigation into the mind and the body, the medieval period seems to be obsessed with demonic influence. What on earth happened between the Romans and our medieval kinfolk?

The reason for the decline in culture, learning and economy is largely credited to the collapse of the Western Empire and the divide between the Latin-speaking West, and Greek-speaking East. Trying to rebuild human knowledge was made difficult by language, civil war, invasion and general decline. No wonder this period is referred to as the Dark Ages…

Medieval

Although the legacy gifts of this period include universities, glasses, and the Magna Carter, the Medieval period largely ignored the wonders of the mind, probably as they were still trying to rebuild the realms of knowledge and learning. At this point, people were more concerned with demonic influence than reasonable science-based enquiries of the mind.

Modern age (1500 – present day)

Renaissance

No wonder the Renaissance is often known as the 'Age of Discovery'. The Renaissance can be likened to an awakening after the long and terrible Dark Ages; new thinking, rediscoveries and vast leaps in knowledge were the order of the day.

Enlightenment

The Enlightenment gave us not only huge leaps and bounds in science, but also in philosophy too. Descartes, Kant, Locke and Voltaire were all kicking about and doing some serious thinking about thinking at this time. This means that around now, the mind was considered as the key to good physical health and with around 70% of visits to the GP today having a psychological basis, these guys weren't far from the mark.

The Victorians

Our final historic snapshot comes from our industrious Victorian friends. The Victorians invented loads of stuff like the tube, post boxes and sewing machines. However, as the era also gave us words like Bedlam, and lunacy reform, it is clear that the Victorians did little to help people afflicted with poor mental health. They didn't really do much for anyone who was less than successful either - just ask Oliver Twist.

Bethlem Royal Hospital, or Bedlam, as it is affectionately known, is Europe's first and oldest hospital specialising in mental illness. During the later stages of the Victorian era, the treatment of mental illness moved away from physical restraint, toward 'moral management' and a system of reward and punishment. This snappy little movement was known as 'Lunacy Reform' and was triggered by an investigation that found many patients chained up, naked, and being treated like animals. So, things have moved on a bit since then...

The rise of the robots

As long ago as 1637, we have been concerned by the development of machines that can think for themselves. There are even numerous novels and films that take this idea on and develop it into a frightening vision of the future in which we puny humans are controlled by scary robots. But how close are we in reality to a population of fully sentient, conversing, self-aware robot overlords?

Right now, we live in a world where we happily converse with AI on a daily basis through our phones and the virtual assistants that help us to navigate the online world – some more successfully than others. We work alongside robots in the manufacturing industries and sometimes we even undergo surgery carried out with robotic assistance, too. *Twitter bots, Machine learning, Big Data, algorithms* are all words we need to understand are in fact examples of artificial intelligence that control much more than we think. Many scientists argue that we are at least fifty years away from the intelligent robots of our nightmares but, in reality, AI is already here and changing the world in which we live.

Robots are 'things' and we understand that 'things' cannot be hurt, don't feel and don't think. But when robots start to be capable of responding to their environment (protecting themselves from extreme heat and so on), using emotional phrasing and emotional facial expressions, where do we draw the line between 'thing' and 'being'?

We already have computers that can win at complex games like Go and chess and even the scientists that created them do not fully understand how they work or how they arrive at a particular game-play strategy. What is reassuring is that these examples are restricted to one particular function and cannot interact with humans.

So how are going to know when to get grovelling to our future robot masters? Or rather, how are we going to know that we have created a sentient machine?

The Turing test

Is there no end to the amazing abilities of Alan Turing? Not only was he a maths genius, but he virtually invented modern computing as well as the Enigma Code Breaker which helped the Allies to win the Second World War. As well as all this, he also invented what has become known as the Turing Test. Developed by Turing in 1950, the test is designed to test a machine's ability to behave in a manner indistinguishable from human beings. Essentially, the test would be passed if, in the course of a text-based conversation between a human and a machine, the evaluator could not tell which participant was the machine and which was the human.

Every year, there is an annual Turing test competition known as the Loebner Prize.[6] The prize awards programmers who have created the most human-like machine. Judges carry out the assessment just as Turing prescribed: they carry out text-based conversations with a human and a machine via a screen and try to work out which is which.

While there has been an annual winner for the most *human-seeming* program, there are also two prizes that have *never* been awarded and are considered one-time-only events. The first is for a program that cannot be distinguished from a real human at all and that manages to convince the judge that the human is a computer program. The second is for a program that passes a full Turing test including de-

---

6. http://www.aisb.org.uk/events/loebner-prize

ciphering and understanding text, visual and auditory input. When there is a winner for these prizes, the competition will end (as well might humanity itself).

In conclusion, how will we know when we are at the mercy of our robot leaders? We probably won't...

Today

The current use of the word 'mind' to refer to our mental powers like memory, choice, thinking and feeling gradually developed between 1300-1400. This means that over time, we humans have come to slowly but surely understand exactly what it is that makes us tick. Or have we?

It can be argued that the treatment of mental health problems has never been more modern. Yet underfunding, a lack of understanding and the social issues that often accompany mental health issues make for a stubbornly confusing state of play. Whilst many people would rather not experience the unusual treatments of yesteryear, there remains a lot of development and progress to be made in the realm of mental health care.

WHAT DOES THE MIND DO FOR US?

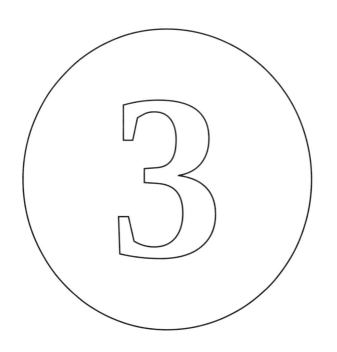

Our minds are truly wonderful things. Not only do they allow us to function in the world, experience beauty and great stuff like love and joy, but they also do some pretty fab things for us too. Our minds give us sleep, dreams and memory - possibly the greatest of all our human being skills.

Sleep

Sleep is a weird thing, not only does it account for approximately 20 years of our lives, but it also a time when our minds really get out to play. Our sleep each night runs in cycles through a series of stages of REM and non-REM sleep numerous times over the course of an average night. Sleep is restorative, helps to protect and improve memory and generally makes us feel really good.

Non-REM sleep has three main categories ranging from light-sleep to slow-wave sleep. It is the deepest sleep we reach and the bit that we need to keep our brains and bodies healthy. Many scientists believe this part of our sleep prevents the build-up of toxins in our brains. Non-REM sleep is categorised by The American Academy of Sleep Medicine as N1, N2, and N3.[7] Each night we cycle through all the stages of sleep in a regular pattern.

During the REM sleep stage, roughly 90 minutes after falling asleep, our minds are busy practising new tasks such as learning to play a piece of music, riding a bike, playing a sport or other procedural tasks. This stage is characterised by rapid eye movement (hence the name), inconsistent breathing, an increased and irregular heart rate, and muscular paralysis – freaky stuff. This phase lasts for up to 30 minutes per cycle or around 25% of your total sleep each night.

7. http://www.sleepeducation.org

While many mysteries remain in the realm of sleep, what is clear is that sleep deprivation has a devastating impact on our bodies and can increase the risk of developing high blood pressure, diabetes, obesity, heart disease and depression. Just ask any brand new parents (then give them a nice mug of cocoa and offer to take the baby off their hands for an hour or two).

Our sleep is controlled by our Circadian clocks. The Circadian clock releases hormonal signals based on environmental cues to create a day time/night time rhythm. Keeping our clocks regular has a positive effect on our sleep patterns. It is recommended that adults aim for between 7-9 hours of sleep per night but the modern world often makes this difficult, which can lead to problems. Humans thrive on a regular sleep-schedule which is why, as tempting as it may be, that sleep-in at the weekend is not actually a good idea.

Dreams

Dreams are weird aren't they? A crazy selection of thoughts, images, people, places, and feelings all whizzing about seemingly randomly that can have you waking up believing you have killed someone, or feeling like you've just brought world peace *and* had a go on a spaceship. But what exactly are dreams?

Freud believed that dreams were a fascinating peak into our unconscious mind and lots of scientists think that dreams are the way our brains organise that days' events, thoughts, and experiences. Dreaming does seem to be highly symbolic such that dreaming about being trapped in a cave away from society can relate to real-life feelings of being ostracised from friends and so on.

Dreams are crazy events chained together in a puzzling way and are best remembered during REM sleep, which is why our muscles are paralysed during this phase, otherwise we would be acting out all of our wildest night time escapades. Some people don't remember their dreams at all, while others are frequent sharers of what they dreamed the night before.

In reality, the big cinematic dreams we experience might only last for a couple of minutes which means our dream time can be packed and mess with our sense of time and space. We spend about two hours of our sleep dreaming and there is no limit to what your mind can conjure up at this time. What seems insignificant and ignored during the day can be recalled in a dream for no apparent reason.

Memory

Though we like to think of the memory as a distinct area of the brain, just like the mind, in reality what we refer to as 'memory' is actually a process that organises how we store and recall information. Memory gives us the ability to learn and to plan, and is the process through which we process huge amounts of data from our experiences, images we see, sounds we hear, and well, you get the picture.

The Atkinson-Shiffrin Memory Model is a 1968 model of how we store and use memory. The model specifies three types of memory: sensory register, short-term store and long-term store.

Short term and long term memories are stored in different ways. While long term memories make actual physical changes to our brains, short-term memories are linked to the electrical activity in our neurons. Scientists have also found that short-term memory works best when we have about seven topics or chunks to grapple with (we can keep a whole lot more related information within each chunk). This could have implications if you are heading toward exam season, or even off to the supermarket.

Long term memory, or declarative memory, involves knowing facts and doing well in pub quizzes and is how we consciously recall things like the dog's birthday and the capital of Belize. Another aspect of long-term memory is procedural memory which is very durable and can withstand serious mental incapacitation such as Alzheimer's. This stores our own personal 'how-to' manual and helps us to remember how to do things that call on our motor skills like tie our shoes or play the flute.

Memories triggered by smell are thought to be more emotionally rich so if you are really trying to commit something important to memory, it might be good to keep something you can smell on hand that you can use to trigger the retrieval of that memory at a later date.

HOW TO IMPROVE YOUR MIND

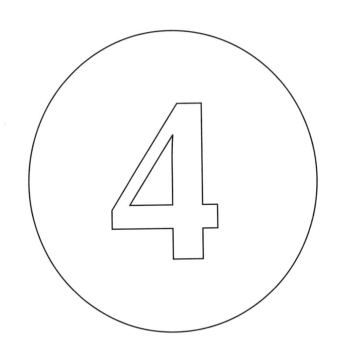

The human brain is thought to produce as many as 12,000-50,000 distinct thoughts per day – no wonder the brain uses 30% of your calorie intake to keep itself fuelled up and ready to think. If you wanted to *improve* your mind though, how might you go about it?

There are generally three areas to consider when people talk about improving the mind. First is the reduction of stress and anxiety, secondly the improvement of memory and, finally, increasing brain power.

Reducing stress

One of the best ways known to reduce stress and anxiety is the practice of Meditation. Meditation releases mood-boosting endorphins and fMRI scans have repeatedly shown that meditation helps your brain to relax by switching off the bits that are dealing with you and your relationship to the world around you. This has a positive effect as it allows the brain to be less anxious about new experiences, increases our levels of compassion and can boost creativity and memory recall.

Getting enough sleep is vital when it comes to general well-being. Simply put, we do not do well if we aren't getting enough sleep – more on which later.

Other activities that have the X-Factor when it comes to making us more at one with ourselves are reading and taking actual time off. Modern work demands more and more from us, but it is so important to remember that all work and no play makes Johnny and Jane very stressed out indeed.

Boosting memory

At some time in our lives, we become very interested in boosting our memory for one reason or another. Remember all those brain training apps? This is one trend that seems to have died a death after the initial excitement, due in part to actual scientific research. Evidence suggests that while they can improve your skills in carrying out the specific tasks associated with that game, they do not improve overall cognitive ability. Sorry, no easy fix to be found here.

One way to boost your memory is to practice paying attention. Focus on the new thing you are learning, whatever it may be. Think about it, run the information through your mind again and let it assimilate. Be conscious in your efforts to process new things and your efforts will really pay off.

Another strategy is to rehearse, revise and revisit. If you are trying to learn something new like a language, concept, or instructive task like a new sport or instrument, then repeating the action or information as many times as you can in as many ways as you can is very effective.

A final suggestion borne from research is to get your senses involved. It has been shown that memories triggered by smell are the most powerful. If you are trying to improve your memory in general, then try to associate the new thing you are trying to store with some sensory data. For example, when you meet a new person, before their name goes flying off into the ether, what can associate with their name? Perhaps their name might offer a clue, which is great if your new friend is called Rose, but less helpful if they go by a less visual name, like Steve.

Brain power

Trying to boost brain power is a tricky issue. But there are a number of strategies that have been shown to improve the actual function of the brain, and a few things that have not. In general, the following tips are good and safe choices to make when it comes to trying to give your brain a bit of a leg-up.

Learn a musical instrument:

Music isn't just lovely to listen to, scientists have shown that musicians also have significant changes to the brain. For example, musical folk have a larger corpus callusum, the bundle of nerve fibres that connects the left and right hemispheres. They also have larger areas of the brain that deal with movement, spatial awareness, and depending on the instrument, touch sensation. So if you want a serious bit of brain boosting, dust off your school recorder and get playing.

Avoid stress:

Early stress, abuse, neglect and harsh treatment not only increase the risk of some physical conditions like obesity, but also increase the risk of people developing depression and anxiety. Keeping stress levels down and life flowing smoothly isn't always in our ability to control, but it can make a difference. Learning how to cope when the odds are stacked against you is a good way to protect your brain from unnecessary strain – little wonder that resilience is the buzz word of the moment.

Eat brain boosting foods:

Omega-3 oils found in fish, flaxseed, walnuts, spinach and broccoli have been proven to improve brain health. A good variety of fruit and veg also helps to protect the brain from damage thanks to the levels of antioxidants contained in them. And to wash down all that goodness, try green tea and moderate amounts of wine. Be careful though, remember that alcohol kills brain cells. On that note, you should also avoid food preservatives, dyes and other additives. Doing so can improve IQ test performance by 14%.

Exercise your body:

Exercising has long been proven to reduce stress, increase energy levels and generally make you feel better by elevating your feel good hormones. A daily walk or a quick jog round the park releases endorphins, chemicals produced in the body that work a little bit like morphine – no wonder some people get addicted to running.

Keep learning:

Learning new things is good for us in all sorts of ways – but you probably already know this because you have chosen to read this very book. Keep those neurons firing, changing, and connecting by learning new things throughout your life. Always wanted to learn to play the piano? Give it a go. How about learning a language, or how to paint? Pack your bags, or pick up that paint brush, your brain will thank you for it.

Don't forget your second brain

More and more studies are turning to the importance of taking care of your gut flora in order to improve your general health, as well as your brain function. Eating a diverse range of fruit and veg, and boosting your fibre intake makes for a healthy diet. You can also boost the number of good bacteria in your gut by having a nibble of fermented foods like kimchi and sourdough bread as these have been shown to improve the makeup of our gut bacteria in some studies. Because there are 100 million neurons that call our stomachs home, bacteria have been thought to influence our behaviour and reduce the risk of all sorts of diseases hence the gut becoming known as the 'second' brain.

WHEN THINGS GO WRONG

Mental health problems

Having good mental health is something that most of us take for granted, most of the time. A sense of emotional, psychological and social wellbeing is the norm for most people. However, sometimes things get out of hand and this is where we can start to exhibit signs of mental health problems that can affect how we see ourselves in relation to the rest of the world and how we behave within our friendships and other relationships.

While being able to cope with the swings and roundabouts of life is a sign of resilience, mental health illnesses can make being able to cope a much more difficult prospect. Increased anxiety, sleeplessness and problematic thoughts that interfere with normal life and continue for a few weeks can indicate a mental health disorder.

The most common mental health disorders are depression, stress and anxiety, psychosis, eating problems, obsessive-compulsive disorder (or OCD) and personality disorders. It is thought that around 1 in 4 people will experience difficulties with their mental health at some point in their lives.[8]

It's just as important to take care of your mental health as it is to keep your physical self in tip-top condition. Having a supportive social network (of the real-life variety as opposed to the online), the ability to share problems with your family and friends and knowing the signs of a problem to look out for are good ways to ensure you are doing your best to look after your own mental health.

If you feel that your mental health could do with a bit of an M.O.T., head to the GP in the first instance.

---

8. https://www.mind.org.uk/information-support/types-of-mental-health-problems/mental-health-problems-introduction/#.WpawvGacbUI

Addiction

Problems with addiction are often associated with mental health illness and vice versa. According to the NHS, there are currently approximately two million people struggling with an addiction. For many people struggling with an addiction, poor mental health is often a root cause as sufferers turn to other substances such as alcohol and drugs in order to feel better. In return, long-term addiction to particular substances can also trigger problems with mental health making the whole situation a perpetual cycle that is exceptionally difficult to break.

Addiction is classified as having a dependence on a substance whether it be illegal or otherwise. The most common addiction is smoking. Nicotine is the fifth most addictive substance on Earth and because it is legal and readily available, it is also one of the hardest addictions to break – just ask anyone currently trying to give up.

With alcohol in at second place, it is heroin that comes in as the number one most addictive substance. On the Nutt addiction scale, it scores 2.5 out of a maximum score of 3, with 1 in 4 people who try it becoming addicted.[9]

According to the National Institute on Drug Abuse, drugs affect the brain in all sorts of ways but mainly by how they impact on the transmission of neurons (the cells that deliver your brain's messages to the rest of your brain cells). Most drugs also target the brain's pleasure centre and flood your body with dopamine. Because dopamine makes us feel great when released in large doses,

---

9. https://www.addictioncenter.com/community/these-are-the-5-most-addictive-substances-on-earth/

taking drugs becomes a reinforced behaviour as we want to take them again and again in order to replicate those good feelings. We are hardwired to repeat activities that we associate with pleasure and reward and our brains teach us to seek out that feeling sub-consciously.

The problems come, however, when we have to take more and more of a substance in order to reach that same initial high. Be-cause the brain releases less dopamine as we get used to a sub-stance, users need more of it in order to achieve that same feeling. Factor in the problem that most addictive substances are either medically controlled, or illegal, and that's where addicts start to run into problems.

Long term drug addiction or use can make structural changes to the brain. Because dopamine's ability to act on the reward centres of the brain reduces with long term substance abuse. This means users feel abnormally flat, low and depressed when they are not under the effects of the drug they are addicted to. Additional prob-lems such as cognitive impairment and changes to nonconscious memory systems that cause reflexive cravings can also occur.

Again, if some of this sounds scarily familiar or is affecting some-one you know and love, head to the GP as the first port of call. There are also a number of excellent helplines you can call for more information and guidance.

Things we used to think would work

Through time, there have been all sorts of wacky ways to think about the mind.

- Way back when, Buddha described the mind as being filled with drunken monkeys that each characterised a different aspect of the mind. He argued that fear was perhaps the most badly behaved of all the monkeys. According to him, meditation could calm the monkeys.

- The CIA conducted experiments using LSD as a way to completely wipe the minds of retiring CIA agents.

- Phrenology, or the study of the shape and size of your head, was discredited by 1840. Prior to this, Franz Joseph Gall concocted the idea that the lumps and bumps on your skull could explain the brain beneath it – how it works, your mood and how you behave could all be determined by the shape of your skull.

- It was thought that lobotomy, or cutting chunks out of your actual brain, could cure mental illnesses like schizophrenia – it certainly cannot!

- There is a hard-core group of people out there who strongly believe that trepanation – or drilling holes into your skull – can give you all sorts of health benefits. Despite these dubious modern claims, what trepanation was originally designed to do was to cure people of demonic possession.

- If trepanation wasn't bad enough, a further very early treatment for mental health issues was exorcism and prayer. Such ceremonies were meant to relieve sufferers and their families of the problem of being possessed by demons. Really.

- How about a spot of mesmerism? Does that sound good? Mesmerism was invented by the father of hypnotism, Franz Mesmer in the late 18th Century. He decided mental health conditions were controlled by the gravitational pull of the moon acting upon the body's fluids (yes, really). In order to counteract this gravitational pull, Mesmer extolled the virtues of magnets to re-distribute bodily fluids and restore harmony in the mind.

- How about an ice bath for your mental health condition? No? Okay then, physical restraints until you feel better? Hmm... These dubious strategies were commonly used in the 18th century to treat mental illness.

And finally, perhaps the most dangerous of all these 'therapies', the late 1800s saw the rise of fever therapy where patients with a mental health illness were exposed to another physical condition associated with high fever such as malaria, in the hope that the fever would see off the original illness.

WEIRD FACTS ABOUT THE MIND

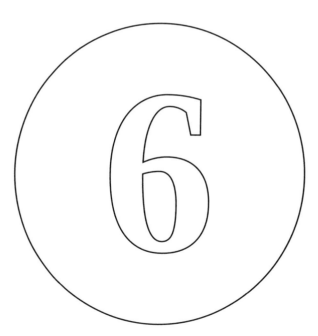

- Our minds are off on their own wanderings for around 30% of the time. When we're driving long boring distances, such as on a motorway, this increases to 70% – which is somewhat alarming.

- Synaesthesia: This is a condition where one sense stimulates another one. This means smells can be sensed as colours, numbers can be sensed as colours and all kinds of other interesting manifestations.

- You can create false memories by tying sensory information to repeated phrases e.g. meeting Superman at Disneyland (which is not possible as he is a Marvel rival) can be made into a false memory if the subject is asked repeated questions about the meeting, and is then invited to imagine the experience on a sensory level e.g. the feeling of touching his cape.

- Nature and nurture is a real thing: there are over a hundred studies that have shown that crime is caused half by genetic factors, and half by environmental factors such as parenting and poverty.

- Films, TV, advertisers and shops all take advantage of the mind in order to get us to engage with the product or text at hand. Simple things like scent association can make us buy certain products in the supermarket. For example, if we smell fresh bread being baked, we are more likely to buy some delicious baked goods. Cultural texts make regular use of product placement in order to serve as subconscious marketing. For example, if James Bond wears a particular watch, we may feel that we can be just like him if we buy the watch concerned.

- The canonical perspective tells us that the mind views things slightly from above and offset to the left or right. When asked to draw a coffee cup from memory, participants unanimously drew it from a position slightly above the cup and looking down – none of them drew it straight on.

- The mind helps us to block out certain sensory information such as the smell of our own perfume, or the feeling of our clothes against the skin. If it didn't, we would be distracted by sensory input and wouldn't be able to focus on anything else.

- Speaking of the connection between our minds and our bodies, it is thought that upwards of 60% of visits to the GP are borne out of psychological reasons.

- It is possible to reduce pain by tricking the mind e.g. viewing a wound through the wrong end of a telescope or magnifying glass can reduce pain levels by making the injury seems smaller.

- Mirrors have been proven very effective in relieving problems associated with phantom limb syndrome. In amputee patients, it is common to find that the missing limb continues to cause pain that can be relieved, reduced, or eradicated by using a mirror box so the patient can view a reflection of the present limb as though it is the missing limb. This allows the brain to relax the nerves muscles and tendons that are still trying to move the missing section.

HOW DO
WE STUDY
THE MIND?

Psychology is essentially the study of the mind. How we perceive the world, how we interact with others, our motivations and how we understand ourselves are all topics of interest to psychologists all over the world.

Because psychologists cannot see inside our minds, after all, all that is visible is the actual brain matter itself, how do they go about studying the mind and all its fascinating mysteries?

Just as many areas of scientific interest are invisible to the naked eye, so psychologists must devise experiments, tests and studies that examine the affect the mind has on the world. And how does the mind impact the world? Through human behaviour.

Schools of thought

There are six main schools of thought in the history of psychology in the west and knowing a little bit more about each one can tell reveal a lot about how we have thought of the mind through time. Sometimes thought of as classic theories of psychology, each of these schools gives us a big name in the world of psychology all of whom have shaped and moulded the science that we know and understand today.

Structuralism

Structuralist psychologists wanted to study the structure of the mind and break it down into its component parts. Though breaking down such an abstract idea seems impossible today, Structuralists were the first scientists to make psychology an independent area of scientific study and established the scientific approach to the field as well. One such Structuralist, Wilhelm Wundt opened the very first psychology lab in Germany in 1879.

Functionalism

Leading directly on from Structuralism came Functionalism. Functionalists believed that studying the function of the mind, rather than the structure would help us to understand how it all worked. Functionalists like Edward B. Titchener were more interested in how and why we engage our mental functions. Functionalists were the first psychologists to study abnormal behaviour and the minds of children and animals and, because of this, they brought the whole field on in leaps and bounds.

Behaviourism

Behaviourists, like John B. Watson, believe that human behaviours are learned from the environment around us and that the forces that control the mind come from the environment and the contexts in which we live. The Behaviourists only studied external, observable behaviour.

Psychoanalysis

Psychoanalysis is the big hitter when it comes to the history of psychology. Thanks to Sigmund Freud, most adults have some sort of understanding of the theories that underpin Psychoanalysis. In fact, most adults would also associate Freud with the whole topic of psychology overall. Freud was interested in the unconscious mind and thought of the human mind as an iceberg e.g. only part of it was visible to other people and most of it remained hidden. Freud steered psychology toward the study of what lay beneath, or the unconscious triggers that underscore our public behaviour. There is no doubt that Freud is the Grandfather of psychology. He was the first to write about it so extensively and his work is the starting point for much advancement in the study of the mind today.

Humanistic

Humanist psychologists, like Carl Rogers, were very interested in the concept of the 'self' and placed importance on values, intentions and meaning. Rather than being controlled by either the unconscious mind as per Psychoanalysis, or by the environment as per Behaviourists, Humanistic psychologists view humans as free to control their own lives and as inherently good in nature.

Cognitive

Cognitivists, such as Jean Piaget, are concerned with how the mind operates and processes information. They liken the mind to a computer that inputs, stores, and retrieves data. They also suggest that a mediational process exists between stimulus (from the environment) and response. Cognitive psychology says that if we want to understand the motivations, impulses and actions of a person, we must understand the processes going on inside the mind. Cognitive psychology is probably the most prevalent school of thought at work today as well as giving rise to one of the more commonly used psychological therapies, Cognitive Behavioural Therapy, or CBT.

Areas of Psychology

There are numerous areas of study that are of interest to psychologists. Amongst these are abnormal, forensic, developmental, comparative and biological.

Abnormal psychology is the study of abnormal behaviour, mental disorders and often works in tandem with psychotherapy to treat people with serious mental illness.

Forensic psychology works within the legal system and psychologists might work in the prison system, the police force, law firms and government agencies.

Developmental psychologists study human growth and development over the average human lifespan from cradle to grave.

Comparative psychology is the study of animal behaviour and how it might help us to understand human behaviour.

Biological psychologists explore how genetic profile and physiology affect our thoughts, feelings and behaviour.

Famous studies of the mind

Hold onto your hat, what follows are some seriously explosive psychological experiments that really changed the way we think about the mind.

Stanford Prison Study, 1971

A team of researchers at Stanford University, under psychologist Philip Zimbardo, recreated a prison scenario made up of twenty-four students of sound mind and clear of any criminal convictions. Prisoners, who were kept in cells 24-hours a day, and guards, on 8-hour shifts, were observed using hidden cameras. After just six days, the experiment was halted due to the abusive and extreme behaviour of the 'guards'. Zimbardo revealed that the guards stripped the prisoners, put bags over their heads and made them participate in humiliating sexual activities.[10] And the moral of this story? With very little encouragement, we all have it within us to become evil tormenters.

Stanford Marshmallow Experiment, 1960

Another example of the Stanford drive to understand the mind, this experiment tests the ability of children to delay instant gratification. Four-year old children were left alone in a room with one marshmallow on a plate. They were told that they could either eat the marshmallow straight away or if they could wait for fifteen minutes, they could have two. While most of the children caved and gave into the delights of instant gratification, those who did manage to resist helped to further our understanding that delayed gratification is associated with lower rates of obesity, drug addiction and behavioural problems.

The Harvard Grant Study 1938 onward

It turns out, The Beatles were right all along; love *is* all you need. One of the most comprehensive and long-running psychological studies tracked male Harvard graduates for 75 years concluding that love is the key element when it comes to finding long-term happiness and a living a fulfilled life. The study also concluded

---

10. Zimbardo, Philip: The Lucifer Effect, (Random House, 2007)

that warm relationships with your parents lead to all sorts of positive effects on adults such as lower rates of dementia, better holidays and higher earnings – go parents!

The Milgram Experiment, 1974

The Milgram Experiment was carried out in order to understand how and why people obey. Couched in trying to understand how justifications for genocide were offered at the Nuremberg War Criminal trials, Stanley Milgram split 40 participants into either learner or teacher roles. The learner was strapped to a chair rigged with electrodes and given facts to learn. The teacher was instructed to shock the learner every time he made a mistake. If the teacher refused to administer the shock, a further participant, in the role of the experimenter, issued commands for them to continue. All the teachers administered shocks to their learners, but only a few refused to administer the highest shock level. This experiment showed that we tend to obey orders from those in authority and that obedience is ingrained in us in childhood.

The Backfire Effect, 2016

The brilliantly named Brain and Creativity Institute at The University of Southern California, conducted a study in which participants were presented with counterarguments to their dominant political beliefs. This happened as the participants were inside an MRI machine and as such, scientists were able to conclude that the amygdala responds to physical and intellectual threat. This means that we are hard-wired to respond to intellectual threat in the same way that we would respond to a big scary dog trying to attack us. What this ultimately means is that our core beliefs are very difficult to challenge given that they are unyielding and inflexible. This might go someway to help explain the divisiveness of current political situations (not naming any names... Brexit and Trump).

Where are we today?

Today, psychology is a huge area of scientific study and psychologists may use an assortment of approaches from the myriad schools of thought in order to achieve their goal. Psychologists use their extensive training and clinical skills to help their patients to better cope with life or mental health difficulties.

People see a psychologist for help with all sorts of problems from the temporary to the chronic. They might employ medicine, talk therapy, hypnotherapy or cognitive behavioural therapy (CBT) amongst other things, to help their patients to overcome their problems and learn to cope better with the stresses of the modern world. Psychologists can work with individuals, families, couples, children – you name the problem, there is a psychologist out there to help.

LIFE AFTER DEATH

DEATH

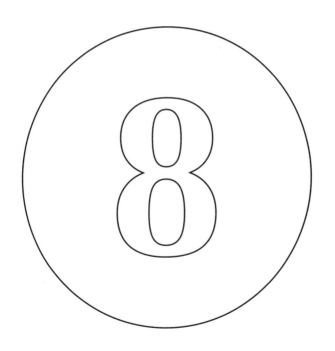

Cryonics

Have you ever thought about what will happen to you after you cross the threshold of those pearly gates? You may have thought about what happens to your body and all your worldly riches, but what about your mind and your brain?

How about a spot of cryonics? At last, you have the opportunity to live your life knowing that when the time comes and it's game over, your body will simply be frozen and in many years, you will be thawed out and ready to go all over again.

Cryonics is the science of freezing bodies at the point of death, storing them in a cryogenic vessel, and then reanimating them later on.

The first problem with the cryonics process is that human bodies just don't respond very well to being frozen and then defrosted – just ask any mountaineer with a few missing fingers and toes. When cells freeze, they fill with ice crystals which then expand causing catastrophic damage to the cell wall.

The second problem is that there is still so much we don't understand about the mind and consciousness that we cannot be sure (at this point in time at least) that we would be 'ourselves' upon re-animation. If our personalities, our 'selves' are formed in the connections of our brains, what damage might occur to these sensitive areas during both the freezing and thawing processes?

The trouble is, we are so far away from even beginning to figure out how to defrost human beings that the likelihood of cryonics being a viable option seems like a dim and distant dream. Then factor in the current impossibility of reversing the ageing process, coupled with curing whatever it was that killed them in the first place, and you begin to see what a challenging area of scientific advancement this really is.

There are a number of rumoured guests of companies that specialise in cryonics but perhaps the most well-known is Walt Disney. However, Mr Disney was *not* frozen when he died and was in fact cremated according to a number of sources.[11] The first person to have themselves cryonically frozen was Dr. James Bedford, a retired psychology professor, in 1967.[12]

The thing is though, is it really such a sci-fi idea?

For a number of years, a form of freezing has been used to prevent further brain injury during incidences of oxygen deprivation. People who suffer from cardiac arrest or heart-attack, have their core temperatures lowered in a process known as therapeutic hypothermia, or targeted temperature management, in order to prevent the development of neurological problems caused by a lack of oxygen to the brain. After resuscitation, the patient is cooled to between 32-34°C.

It is also used on tiny babies. Babies who suffer hypoxic-ischemic encephalopathy (HIE) at birth (or in other words, are starved of oxygen), are deliberately cooled via therapeutic hypothermia in order to protect oxygen-starved brain tissue and allow it to regenerate. This is a growing area of medical research at present but when used, it can reduce the instances of life-changing disabilities.[13]

So, what might once have seemed like a crazy science fiction story, now has some relevance to medical advancement today.

11. http://entertainment.time.com/2013/10/16/10-things-you-probably-didnt-know-about-walt-disney/

12. http://www.alcor.org/Library/html/BedfordSuspension.html

13. http://www.aboutkidshealth.ca/En/News/NewsAndFeatures/Pages/Cooler-heads.aspx

Brain bank

Did you know that after your death, you can donate your brain to one of the network of brain banks we have in the UK?

Led by the Medical Research Council, the UK Brain Bank Network is an initiative designed to coordinate UK brain tissue resources for researchers. There are a number of brain banks all over the country and if you want to donate your brain for the advancement of scientific and medical research, you can simply get in touch with your nearest one or to put it another way, the future home of your brain.

Scientists use donated brain tissue from healthy and diseased brains in order to research a number of neurological conditions such as dementia, Alzheimer's, Parkinson's, multiple sclerosis, autism, Huntington's, motor neurone disease, and a number of psychiatric disorders. Your donated brain might become part of research into genetic disorders, or neurological diseases and could help millions of people in the future. There are currently 12 million people living with a neurological condition and this figure is only going to rise as the population continues to age so brain research has never been more important.

If you opt to donate your brain, as long as the donation occurs within 72 hours of death, the whole brain is removed along with a portion of the brain stem, and possibly some cerebrospinal fluid too. All you have to do is register your wish to donate prior to the end of your life, and then ensure that your GP and loved ones know of your intention. Upon your death, they will then contact the relevant brain bank.

Brains that have been affected by a neurological condition are of most use to researchers, but healthy brains are also needed to act as controls in scientific experiments. In fact, because brain banks are relatively unknown, there is a shortage of healthy tissue as, commonly, donors are much more likely to have come across the bank network during treatment for neurological issues. For perhaps the more grizzly-minded amongst you, you may like to know that the removal of the brain does not cause any disfigurement to the body of the deceased.

Once the brain is removed, half of it is stored in a cryogenic -80°C freezer to preserve it, the other half is used to make a definitive diagnosis as to the neurological issue concerned. The tissue remains viable for research for ten years so it really is a great legacy to consider.[14]

Messages from beyond the grave

A trip to the seaside just isn't complete without the reassuring existence of an overly decorated Madam someone-or-other's mysterious medium or clairvoyance booth. There are a great many people who make a seriously good living from their apparent ability to receive and decode messages from beyond the grave but is there any truth to it?

Mediums often explain that their 'gift' became apparent when they were still a child; perhaps they experienced some paranormal event or happening. Upon adulthood, they became able to distil their gift, refining it to become a medium between this life and the next. Some mediums claim to have a spirit guide who communicates directly with the dead and translates their messages to them. Some claim to work solo. There are many people who find spiritualists incredibly reassuring, and many more who find them exploitative con-artists.

---

14. https://www.mrc.ac.uk/research/facilities-and-resources-for-researchers/brain-banks/donating-brain-and-spinal-cord-tissue/

So what does the mind have to do with messages from beyond the grave? According to science, absolutely nothing.

MYSTERIES OF THE MIND

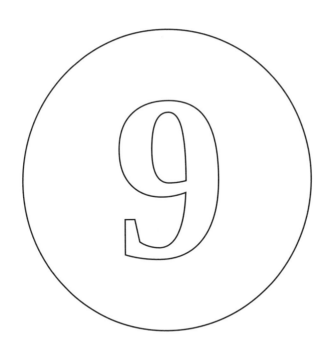

Nature vs. nurture

Throughout time, we have pondered upon the great nature / nurture debate. Are evil folk born that way, or did their early lives somehow make them turn out bad?

This links to debates surrounding the very nature of our characters, what makes us who we are? Is it genetic? Our upbringing? Our peers, or even our education?

Psychologists have shown that nature and nurture are both involved at the scene of the crime as it were. While some of us are genetically predisposed to carrying out acts that are considered 'bad', there are some of us again who have been brought up in an environment that is less than ideal. For some, however, there seems to be no real reason behind poor behaviour. In reality, because we are all the sum of our genetic inheritance *and* our life experiences, there is unlikely to ever be a conclusive answer to this question.

Laughter

Perhaps you have an unusual sense of humour? Or maybe you have a friend who always makes you laugh? Quite possibly, it is, in fact, you who is the joker in the pack made up of your friends and family? What is certain, is that scientists know very little about laughter other than it makes us feel good and that it works on three distinct areas of the brain: the thinking bit, the movement bit, and the emotional bit.

Thanks to the old fMRI scanner, scientists have been able to observe what happens to the brain when we laugh. Unlike other emotional responses that commonly affect just a single area of the brain, laughter seems to travel through the brain working on different areas. First, the left side of the cortex, responsible for language, analyses the words of the 'humour'. Then, the frontal lobe, responsible for emotion, becomes very active, then the right side of the cortex does some serious intellectual analysis. And finally, via the occipital lobe, the motor sections of the brain are activated in order to produce an actual physical laugh.

While we all recognize that laughter truly is the best medicine, what we don't know is why we respond differently. Why is it that a good joke has one person splitting their sides, and another unimpressed beyond belief?

Many researchers have concluded that our sense of humour comes from a combination of our life experiences, our personal value systems, our ages, and our cultural capital. While a bunch of children may laugh uproariously at a fart joke, once we grow up and become adults, we're much more likely to prefer more complex humour, at least, *most* of us that is. It's also commonly the case that it is people who make us laugh – someone caught doing something stupid, or someone we really like trying out a crummy joke is much more likely to make us laugh than if an arch enemy or social nemesis attempts a joke at your expense. In this regard, familiarity in combination with witty observations about the world in which we live is usually the key to the trigger of our laughing muscles.

Laughter has actually been shown to reduce the levels of stress hormones in our bodies, particularly in stressful situations. In a situation where we might be feeling particularly anxious, or scared, laughter actually shuts down the flow of hormones and so can switch off the fight or flight reflex. It also increases the number of good cells that keep us healthy and works with your body's immune response, and can even keep your respiratory tract clear. It even makes for a good workout. A good laughing fit has been shown to equal a ten-minute session on the rowing machine in terms of muscle exercise and increased blood flow.

So, how can you get more laughter into your life? Try taking the time to figure out what it is that makes *you* laugh and do more of it. Go to a comedy club on date night as laughing together has been shown to strengthen relationships and bonds between friends. You could also practice being the funny one – take a stand-up class or learn from the pros, the choice is yours.

Hypnosis

From the early days of film and the infamous *Cabinet of Doctor Caligari*, we have been equally enthralled and repelled by the idea of hypnotism. For two hundred years, we have lived with the knowledge of its existence but as yet, there is very little scientific understanding as to how it actually occurs. Rather than the stereotypical swinging pocket watch of the past, hypnosis today can be a serious part of medical treatments as much as it can form the star attraction of a cabaret act. *But what is hypnosis?*

Hypnosis is a trance-like state characterised by inhibition, relaxation, and heightened imagination. In a stage show, we witness hypnotised audience members participating in all sorts of acts and being open to all sorts of suggestions that they would never consider in their normal lives which is probably why we are so intrigued. While it's funny to see on stage, we can easily imagine it being used for much more nefarious purposes.

You may well have got *yourself* into a kind of hypnotic state. Have you ever set off for work then arrived at your destination seemingly without thinking at any stage? Have you lost yourself in the pages of a good book and been unaware of the real world around you? Have you ever been watching a film and fallen totally into the world depicted such that you give yourself a good scare, or even forget that you are in the cinema or sitting at home on your sofa? If you have, you may have been experiencing a form of self-hypnosis.

In a professional hypnosis session, relaxation and linguistic techniques are used to bypass the conscious mind and get straight at the unconscious mind instead. Because our unconscious mind is busy processing all sorts of things that we aren't even aware of, addressing it via metaphor, patterning, or association is a way of tuning out the rational, critical, analytical conscious mind.

In medical treatment, hypnosis has been used to positively treat a wide range of conditions. A 2007 study showed that hypnosis can drastically reduce the severity and duration of headaches, some dental and surgical treatment is carried out under hypnosis rather than anaesthetic, and hypnosis can also be used to assist in addiction, smoking cessation, and weight management. While our conscious mind may find a million ways to justify an extra piece of chocolate cake or just one more glass of wine, our unconscious mind can be trained to reconsider our sweet-tooth so it can become a more useful weapon in our weight control arsenal.

Can you read my mind?

Another oddity of the mind that has been showcased on the big stage is mind reading. While most of us remain absolutely sceptical about the legitimacy of attempts to read the mind of a stranger, some of us do indeed believe that some people really are 'gifted' in this way.

Sometimes known as mentalism, there are a number of classic tricks that make people believe their mind is, in fact, being 'read'. The classic elephant trick, the ashes on the arm trick, many card tricks, and the touch head mind reading trick all largely rely on mathematics, and physical 'tells' on the part of the 'mark'.

Locked-in syndrome

In all seriousness, however, modern science is developing ways to read the minds of people afflicted with terrible conditions such as locked-in syndrome. Locked-in syndrome is a condition where patients are completely paralysed and unable to talk or even to move their eyes to communicate.

Scientists have already developed a brain-computer interface that deciphers the thoughts of patients by means of analysing their blood oxygen and electrical activity in order to arrive at a simple 'yes' 'no' answer scenario. Patients are asked questions to which there is a simple knowable answer by scientists, such as "your husband's name is George". The patient's electrical activity and brain oxygen levels are then analysed and the process is repeated until a pattern emerges and it becomes clear when a patient is answering positively or negatively. The non-invasive brain-computer interface (or, BCI) has the potential to transform the lives and experiences of patients around the world helping them to communicate with medical professionals and their loved ones. It is hoped that research will continue to develop and that people with all sorts of debilitating conditions such as spinal cord injury, motor neurone disease and paralysis will benefit. Now, this really is mind reading.

Phantom limb disorder

It is thought that around 80% of amputees continue to feel sensations such as pain, temperature changes, itching, and pressure. Understandably, such sensations can often be distressing and can lead to psychological problems concerning their adjustment and normal life. There are a number of theories as to why people may experience phantom limb including the idea that the severed nerve reroutes itself in order to continue sending messages back to the brain, and another that suggests the brain has some kind of electrical map of the body and all its connections. Though it is poorly understood and difficult to treat, doctors are experimenting with all sort of technology – both simple and complex – in order to combat this terrible affliction and improve the lives of amputees.

CONCLUSION

So, there you have it, everything you need to know about the mind in one easy nutshell. You have learned a little bit about the brain and its work, how your brain and mind are connected, as well as a vast plethora of ideas, thoughts about thinking, historical oddities, and weird and wonderful facts about the thing that makes you quintessentially you. You've considered the sentience of our animal sisters and brothers, and contemplated the nightmare future in which we are subservient to our robot emperors – and you've lived to see another day.

Of course, the mind and its workings is a huge topic worthy of years and years of in-depth academic study, and while this little book should give you a taster for what is already known, remember that there are countless volumes that could have been included and this is a field that is continually growing and developing.

Go on and explore the crazy world of the human mind, who knows what you might find out?!

GLOSSARY

Abnormal psychology

The study of abnormal behaviour, and mental disorders – often works in tandem with psychotherapy to treat people with serious mental illness.

AI

Short for 'artificial intelligence' and refers to machines that simulate human intelligence.

Amygdala

The part of the brain responsible for how we respond to fear and gives us a memory of fear.

Atkinson-Shiffrin Memory Model, the

This is a founding model of how we store and use memory first established in 1968.

Backfire Effect, the

A 2016 study that tested what happens to the brain when it perceives a threat to core beliefs.

Behaviourism

A school of psychological thought that believes human behaviours are learned from the environment and that the forces controlling the mind come from the environment and the contexts in which we live.

Bedlam

An 'affectionate' nickname for Bethlem Royal Hospital, Europe's first and oldest hospital specialising in mental illness.

Biological psychology

The study of how individual genetic profiles and physiology affect our thoughts, feelings and behaviour.

Brainstem

The part of the brain responsible for communication between the brain and the rest of the body.

Canonical perspective

A preferred way of viewing an object that reveals how your mind 'sees' well-known objects.

Cognitive Behavioural Therapy (CBT)

A very popular talking therapy that helps us to explore how we think and act in specific situations.

Cerebral hemisphere

Refers to the halves of the brain – split into the left and right hemispheres that are responsible for different functions. Each hemisphere has four lobes.

Cerebrum

What we think of as the main brain object and contains the two hemispheres that make up the brain.

Cerebellum

The part of the brain inside the cerebrum that regulates movement, posture, balance and coordination.

Circadian clock

An internal clock linked to solar time that controls when we sleep by the production of specific hormones.

Cognitive psychology

This branch of psychology is concerned with how the mind operates and processes information.

Comparative psychology

This branch of psychology studies animal behaviour and how it might help us to understand human behaviour.

Corpus callosum

This is the bundle of nerve fibres that connects the left and right hemispheres.

Developmental psychology

This is the study of human growth and development over a lifespan.

Dunbar's number

First thought of by Robin Dunbar, this refers to the number of people with whom it is possible to maintain a relationship: 150.

False memories

A memory in which a person recalls an event or memory that did not happen as though it were real.

Forensic psychology

This branch of psychology works within the legal system such as the prison system, the police force, law firms and government agencies.

Freud, Sigmund

The founder of psychoanalysis and the most well-known psychologist.

Frontal lobe

This is the part of the brain responsible for self-control, reasoning, planning and abstract thought.

fMRI

Stands for: functional Magnetic Resonance Imaging, this scanner works by charting increased blood flow across the brain.

Functionalism

A school of psychological thought that believed studying the function of the mind rather than the structure was important.

Harvard Grant Study

The longest-running study carried out from 1938 onward. The study explored the key to a happy life with a number of male Harvard graduates.

Hippocampus

The part of the brain in which long-term memories are stored.

Hominid

The collective term for human ancestors such as the Neanderthals.

Homo sapien

The Latin name for the Human Being.

Humanistic

This school of psychological thought was interested in the concept of the 'self' and placed importance on values, intentions, and meaning.

Hypothalamus

The part of the brain that coordinates the brain and the release of hormones.

Lobotomy

Surgery in which part of the brain is removed and an early treatment for mental illness.

Mesmerism

An early treatment for mental illness in which magnets were used to balance the gravitational effect of the moon upon mental health.

Milgram Experiment, the

An experiment carried out in 1974 that tested the human ability to obey authority.

Neurons

These are cells that communicate information from the brain to the rest of the body.

Occipital lobe

This is the part of your brain responsible for vision.

Nutt Addiction Scale

Scores substances out of three according to how addictive they are with three being the most addictive.

Parietal lobe

This is the part of the brain responsible for spatial awareness, navigation and touch.

Phrenology

This is an early idea that posits the shape of the skull as the key to human behaviour and that certain brain functions were located in specific areas.

Piaget, Jean

A cognitive psychologist.

Psychoanalysis

This is the school of psychological thought that studies the unconscious triggers that underscore public behaviour.

REM sleep

A period of sleep characterised by rapid eye movement.

Reticular formation

This is a network of pathways in the brainstem.

Rogers, Carl

A humanistic psychologist.

Social Brain, theory

This theory argues that human intelligence came about as a means of surviving in large social groups.

Stanford Marshmallow experiment

This study tested delayed gratification in children with the use of a marshmallow.

Stanford prison study

This study tested obedience in a false prison setting but was halted after just six days due to the poor behaviour of the participants in the role of the prison guard.

Structuralism

Structuralist psychologists study the structure of the mind and break it down into its component parts.

Synapses

These are the connections that transport neurons.

Synesthesia

A condition in which sensory input is confused such that sufferers may taste colour and so on.

Temporal lobe

This is the part of the brain responsible for processing sensory input, language and communication.

Thalamus

This part of the brain organises and sorts sensory input.

Titchener, Edward. B

One of the first Functionalist psychologists.

Trepanation

An early treatment for mental illness in which holes were drilled into the skull to release demonic influence.

Turing, Alan

The inventor of the Enigma Code Breaker, and the father of modern computing. Turing also invented the Turing Test to assess machine sentience.

Watson, John. B

A Behaviourist psychologist.

Wundt, Wilhelm

One of the first Structuralist psychologists.